WOMEN ARE FROM BRAS
MEN ARE FROM PENUS

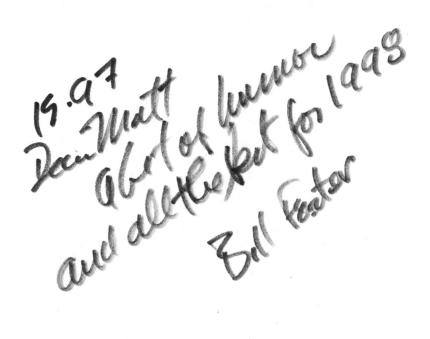

15.97

Dear Matt
a best of humour
and all the best for 1998
Bill Foster

WOMEN ARE FROM BRAS
MEN ARE FROM PENUS

A Survival Guide for
Bypassing Communication and
Getting Even in Your Relationships

Anna Collins, Su.C.*
and
Elliot Sullivan, Su.C.*

Illustrations by Raymond Larrett

Ship of Fools

An Imprint of Sullivan & Foster Publishing, New York
An Entagon Communications Company

*Stand-up Comic

Ship of Fools Books
An Imprint of Sullivan & Foster Publishing
An Entagon Communications Company
173 West 81st Street, Lower Level
New York, NY 10024

Cover and Book Design: Topanga Graphics, Ltd.
ISBN 1-890410-10-1

Books may be ordered in quantity from your local bookseller or you may order single or bulk quantities by phoning:

AES Books
Toll Free: 1-800-717-2669
All credit cards accepted.
E-mail: info@sullivanandfoster.com

This is dedicated to the one I love.

Contents

Acknowledgments

Special thanks to **Michael Panzeca** for his love, patience, understanding, and his ability to prevent Anna from OD'ing on Reese's Peanut Butter Cups; to **Dena Seigel** for her encouragement, support, and creative ideas; to **Peter Coloyan** for his affectionate doubling as an air-traffic controller; to **Michael Wolfsohn** at Topanga Graphics for his design wizardry 59 minutes after the 11th hour; to **Gary Larson** for keeping everything running while all else went to hell; and, above all, special thanks to **Eddie Brill** for introducing Anna and Elliot. If you don't like this book, blame him!

To the Reader

This book is intended as a survival guide and, as such, must go beyond political correctness since human lives are at stake. The battle of the sexes is war, and clearly war is hell.

Nevertheless, there are occasional times when the authors deviate from their cable-ready vernacular and use proper and dignified language without any bias towards either gender. For this we apologize.

If there are not at least one or two lines in this book that rub you the wrong way, the authors question whether you have been reading carefully or just skimming. On the other hand, if you become peeved or upset, this book has clearly hit its mark, and you may want to get extra copies for your friends.

Keep in mind this book is no substitute for the consultation of a licensed health-care professional. Also keep in mind, however, that the consultation of a licensed health-care professional is no substitute for this book.

CHAPTER 1

WOMEN ARE FROM BRAS,
MEN ARE FROM PENUS

NOT THAT LONG AGO in a galaxy not that far away,
lived two opposite civilizations. One lived on the planet Bras and
the other on the planet Penus. Little did they know they were
headed on a collision course for each other. Everybody was
doomed to disaster except the planets' lawyers who, through
personal injury lawsuits, financed their escape while all their
clients went straight to hell.

As the planets got closer and closer, one of the inhabitants on
Penus, a Penusian, was looking through his Penuscope™, which
is like a telescope, only when extended, a lot smaller. He saw the
planet Bras and, much to his delight, spied a bevy of beautiful
bare-bottomed, bosomy Brassierians bathing in brightly
bejeweled bronze bathtubs. After a long series of "B" words, the
Penusian shouted, "Fuckin' A!"

He immediately — after watching for two and a half hours —
called all his buddies to see this incredible sight. The Penusians
started clamoring to get a look at the Brassierians. After taking
many turns watching, the Penusians unanimously decided to take
more turns watching. So they continued watching for several days
until their eyes crossed and their wrists got really really tired.

The Penusians had to meet these gorgeous Brassierians at any cost, unless it meant missing the playoffs on TV. So, being the fix-it-build-it-widget types, they constructed the **Starship Enterthighs** in the hopes they would boldly go where no Penusian had gone before — namely the laundromat.

The Enterthighs was equipped with a 30,000 mhz pentium MMX-K6 computer, a fusion turbo four-hundred-on-the-floor plutonium-injected engine, and a pair of foam dice hanging from the rear-view mirror. It also had a 520-inch remote-controlled TV and a satellite dish capable of receiving 84,329 channels — though there *still* wasn't anything worth watching on TV.

The trip to Bras would have normally taken 3 light years, but it ended up taking 7 because the Penusians were too **egotesticle** to ask other spaceships for directions. Eventually, however, they landed on Bras and everybody had to pee really bad.

The Penusians and Brassierians took to each other right from the start. They were enthralled with each other's differences. Each had something about them that bulged and swelled in a different way. For the Brassierians it was their breasts. For the Penusians it was their egos.

For a while everything went along great because they were madly in love. Love being blind, it wasn't until they got married that they had their eye-opening experience. But, love being blind, they found their way around each other using Braille. This gave rise to sex and things started going along even better. They had great sex, great food, great sex, a little burping and farting here and there, great sex. They couldn't ask for more.

TYPICAL PENUSIAN

Then they all decided to travel to the planet Earth. No one knows for sure why they picked Earth. Some historians think the Brassierians persuaded the Penusians because it was the only planet that had shopping malls. Others feel it was because on Earth, in legal disputes, Penusians would always get the shaft.

Once on Earth, however, they suddenly developed *selective nausea*. They wouldn't be nauseous all the time — only when they were with each other. Pretty soon the touching turned into poking. The poking turned into punching. The punching turned into pounding. And the pounding turned into short-range nuclear weapons.

TYPICAL BRASSIERIAN

To survive they both devised strategies, tactics, schemes, maneuvers, tricks, ploys, games, ruses, gimmicks, deceits, subterfuges, skullduggery and espionage. There were even times when they were subtle and indirect.

Penusians wrote songs about their predicament such as, "A Pretty Girl Is Like A Malady". Brassierians wrote articles in women's magazines such as, "When I Was Dating Him, He Was My Ideal. Now That We're Married, He's My Ordeal".

Books were written as combat manuals. The Brassierians published *The Rules*, a typographical error that is supposed to read, *The Ruse*. Then a bunch of Penusians countered with *The Code*, a typographical error that is supposed to read, *The Cold*, only the person dictating had sinus problems. The Brassierians countered with *Breaking the Rules* while counter-intelligence Penusians responded with *Breaking the Code*. When a Brassierian countered with *The Spy Who Came in from the Cold*, the Penusians finally said, "Gimme a break. I'm getting a cold one!"

....

Men will never understand women and women will never understand men — and that is the one thing that men and women will never understand.

....

Each side tried desperately to understand the other. Penusians tried to understand why Brassierians were interested in the alpha-hydroxy content of their new moisturizer and the best place to get a sugarless double-mocha half-caf cappuccino with fat-free non-diary topping. Brassierians tried to understand why Penusians would be interested in who the new defensive linemen were for the Bills, and who got the most R.B.I.'s in the World Series in 1958.

They tried reading self-help books like, *You Just Don't Understand, How To Enhance Your Interpersonal Communication, What You Thought You Heard Was Not, In Fact, What I Actually Meant,* and finally, *Hey Asshole, What The Fuck Are You Trying To Say?*

What both sides never realized is that men will never understand women and women will never understand men — and that is the one thing that men and women will never understand.

LIFE ON BRAS

Bras is an unusual planet in its ability to retain water. Whenever it rains, the water doesn't evaporate. The planet just soaks it up, swelling to twice its normal size. There are two large mountain ranges on Bras, though each points in a slightly different direction from the other.

Brassierians are not concerned with building highways and tall buildings. They are more concerned with decorating. As a matter of fact, on Bras there are so many throw rugs and throw pillows, you could throw up! Everything on Bras has to match. The couch has to match the rug which has to match the drapes which have to match the paintings which have to match their panties.

And they like to wear a different outfit every day to express how they feel. One day they could be wearing a sexy low-cut red-sequin evening gown, and the next they could be sporting a T-shirt that says, "Fuck You" on the front and "Yeah You!" on the back. They complain they never have anything to wear, and that eight closets aren't enough to hold it.

And Brassierians are also concerned with odors and fragrances. It is clearly the freshest smelling planet in the universe. Nasty odors are a "no-no" and are covered up by an air freshener with a fresh pine scent. When the smell of pine gets too nauseating, it is covered with a new-improved fresh lemony scent. The artificially-engineered, allergic-reaction-producing lemon scent is then covered up with a clear natural scent, though nobody knows what a clear natural scent really smells like. To cover up this chemical wizardry from an olfactory factory, Brassierians scatter baskets of potpourri everywhere — in every hallway and every room, especially in the bathroom. Even the water in the toilet, called toilet water, is colored aqua blue and carries a distinct fragrance to cover up the sickening-sweet smell of the potpourri. And, in case there are any smells they missed, Brassierian post "Stick-Ups", light scented candles, burn incense, use perfume, and wear odor eaters, not just in their shoes, but in any bodily cavity where the sun doesn't shine — such as their nose and ears.

For recreation Brassierians play a lot of games such as bridge, Scrabble, and backgammon — but best of all they like to play dumb. Brassierians also enjoy activities such as shopping. Another pastime they enjoy is shopping with a friend. A third activity they enjoy is shopping with a friend in a mall. A fourth activity they enjoy is "doing lunch". This is especially enjoyable since it can be done while shopping with a friend in a mall.

....

For recreation Brassierians play a lot of games such as bridge, Scrabble, and backgammon — but best of all, they like to play dumb.

....

Brassierians love relating to each other. The only mail that is ever sent is birthday cards and thank-you notes. Then they thank each other for sending the thank-you note. Then they send little stuffed animals as thanks for being thanked, which prompts a thank-you note for the little stuffed animal.

Not a lot gets done on Bras.

LIFE ON PENUS

Penus is just the opposite.

Lots gets done on Penus. The planet is full of power tools, computers, and equipment. Penusians also save small boxes of nuts, bolts, screws, and motor parts that are too old and rusty to use, but too handy to throw out. At least half the planet is covered with these small boxes of motor parts.

Penusians experience fulfillment through success and accomplishment, such as spelling their name in the snow while peeing, or peeking under a woman's skirt without getting caught.

....

Penusians experience fulfillment through success and accomplishment, such as spelling their name in the snow while peeing, or peeking under a woman's skirt without getting caught.

....

Their sense of self is defined by their ability to achieve results — like catching a three-inch minnow with an $850 fishing lure. They value power, competency, efficiency, and achievement, which is why many spend their entire day farting on the couch drinking beer.

....

A Penusian's sense of self is defined by his ability to achieve results — like catching a three-inch minnow with an $850 fishing lure.

....

Penus is a rugged planet. Millions of years ago the entire planet was covered with lush rain forests, though that growth has receded to the point where today there are just scattered clumps of weeds which they let grow to give the appearance of vegetation. There is one tall peak on the planet, though when you get close, it's not as big as you thought it was. Perfectly spherical years ago, the planet now bulges severely at the equator. Known for its volcanic activity, there are thousands of caverns that noisily belch hot gasses that are toxic and smelly.

On Penus toilet seats stay up, milk is solid, and shower curtains have their own eco-system.

On Penus toilet seats stay up, milk is solid, and shower curtains have their own eco-system. Sporting events are very popular and include Olympic Burping, Marathon Crotch Adjusting, and the Dilapidated Underwear Pageant. The phrase "pull my finger" is legend. Competition is keen and there's always some kind of contest going on, such as who can hit the longest golf ball, who can score the most home runs, or who can make the loudest underarm sounds with their hands.

Appearance is also important to a Penusian, and he will often arrive 45 minutes late to work because he was trying to get the dimple right in his tie. Penusians own about 10 suits, though they are all charcoal gray. Hair loss is a major concern to Penusians and they will get hair from any place they can. Whether it comes out of their sideburns, their nose, or their ears, they will let it grow and then flip it over their head. This is called the "swoop method" which has the attractiveness of a man with a mop on his head driving backwards in a convertible doing 100 miles an hour during a hurricane. Another fashionable trend is to tack what little hair he has to his head with wallpaper paste, spray painting any remaining scalp that shows. This creates a look that is as youthful and debonair as Bela Lugosi looked in *Dracula*.

Hair loss is a major concern to Penusians and they will get hair from any place they can. Whether it comes out of their sideburns, their nose, or their ears, they will let it grow and then flip it over their head.

THE LEADER OF BRAS

The leader of Bras is the Goddess WunderBra — an all-knowing, all-seeing, ageless goddess of love with no tolerance for dickheads or schmucks. This mysterious goddess can manifest herself as an angelic intuitive feeling, a secret message in a dream, or an elephantine dish of Häagen-Dazs chocolate-chocolate chip ice cream with hot fudge, chocolate whipped cream, chocolate sprinkles, fresh-shaved chocolate, all lightly dusted with cocoa. Her credo, echoed throughout the entire Brassierian kingdom is, "Do I look fat to you?"

THE GODDESS WUNDERBRA

THE LEADER OF PENUS

The leader of Penus is Penus Maximus, stalwart warrior who stands strong and erect. All Penusians think they are Penus Maximus, though most peter out just before doing battle. This powerful god can manifest as the power to change the course of mighty rivers, bend steel in his bare hands, or flick a remote for 10 straight hours without once enduring a full-length commercial. His credo is, "Do I look cool? Do you live around here?"

PENUS MAXIMUS

CHAPTER 2
MEN FIX EVERYTHING
WOMEN HAVE MEN FIXED

Men and women have all the answers. Too bad they don't have a clue as to what the question is. What is the question? The question is, "Why can't you just shut the hell up?" This, of course, is the one question that never gets answered.

Men and women will spew out nuggets of wisdom that look very similar in size and shape to the nuggets that bulls spew out while they graze.

No matter what the situation, no matter what the circumstance, men and women will spew out nuggets of wisdom that look very similar in size and shape to the nuggets that bulls spew out while they graze.

WOMEN GIVE ADVICE

Women have opinions. Lots of opinions. Opinions about everything. You could say they approach every subject with an open mouth. Women even have opinions that their opinion is "true", not an opinion. Thus, they nag and give advice.

What women do not realize is that to offer a man unsolicited advice is to presume he can't do it on his own. So a woman should never criticize a man. She should call up his 3rd-grade teacher and let *her* criticize him. This way he can respond like the 8-year-old child he really is.

....

A woman should never criticize a man. She should call up his 3rd-grade teacher and let *her* criticize him. This way he can respond like the 8-year-old child he really is.

....

The worst time to criticize a man is when he is driving.

For example, Lulu and Eric are late for a party, and Eric has gotten lost. Eric has turned the trip into a Lewis & Clark Expedition, exploring strange new on-ramps and intersections, driveways leading to nowhere, and cul-de-sacs filled with barking pit bulls. Still, there is a right way and a wrong way for Lulu to handle the situation.

THE WRONG WAY

LULU: Are you sure you know where you're going? We've been driving around in circles for forty minutes! My déja vu is having déja vu.

ERIC: Can I help it if there's no street signs?

LULU: Why don't you ask for directions?

ERIC: Hey, relax! I know where I'm going!

LULU: Yeah, you know where you're going.
Didn't we leave the house last Tuesday?

ERIC: Get off my back!

LULU: You're such an asshole! We're gonna
miss the party and it's all your fault.

Obviously this technique is totally ineffective. Not only do they not find the party, but neither partner scores a decisive victory over the other.

THE RIGHT WAY

LULU: Are you sure you know where you're
going? We've been driving around in
circles for forty minutes!

ERIC: Can I help it if there are no street signs?

LULU: That's okay, sweetie. So what if we get
          there next Thursday. I'm enjoying the
          scenery.

ERIC: We'll find the party, don't worry.

LULU: I'm not worried. I have confidence that if
          I grant you the autonomy that you need,
          your prowess as a driver will rescue us
          from this endless circuitous meandering.
          Besides, I just love gazing at the same
          intersection for the 20th time.

ERIC: Now let's see…do we take this right?
          What do you think?

LULU: Okay, you know what I think? I think you're
          a dumb macho asshole dickhead. Now
          stop the car!

ERIC: What?

*[At this point Lulu pulls out a .38 caliber pistol and points it
at Eric's forehead.]*

LULU: I said, "Stop the car!" Now get out nice and easy
          with your hands in the air and nobody will get hurt.

*[Eric does as she says. Lulu jumps out of the car, hails a cab, and
ends up going to the party with the cab driver.]*

Notice how much more effective this method is. Lulu got to
the party, she dumped a loser, and met someone new. For Lulu
this was a win-win. No one knows what it was for Eric, because
he has never been found.

There is, however, another reason why a woman shouldn't offer a man unsolicited advice. It severely *pisses him off!* and could cause an unexpected adverse reaction.

....

If a woman doesn't put a stop to her little digs, she may end up digging her own grave.

....

HOW A WOMAN CAN NAG A MAN TO DEATH — USUALLY HER OWN!

Nagging a man is a lot of fun and a woman can pick on virtually any detail or bit of minutia at her disposal to make a man feel he's not even worthy of suicide. Because men are slow cookers, however, this can be dangerous, and the surgeon general has warned that continually nagging a man can be hazardous to a woman's health. If a woman doesn't put a stop to her little digs, she may end up digging her own grave.

Here are some examples.

1. **She:** You're working too hard. You should take a day off.

    He: You know, that's so insightful. Maybe you could work 5 times as hard. This way *I* won't have to work at all and in 6 months *you'll* drop dead from a heart attack.

2. **She:** You're not leaving yourself enough time!

    He: You're right. If I gag you, strangle you, and drop you down the elevator shaft, I should allow at least another 15 minutes.

3. **She:** You're driving too fast. Slow down, you'll get a ticket.

He: Thanks for the caution, honey, but in another few seconds I won't be in the car at all, although, when it goes over the cliff up ahead, *you* will be.

4. **She:** Your tool shed is such a mess.

   He: You're so right, honey pie. It should be better organized. When I need my pick ax, chain saw, and sling blade, I need to find them in a hurry.

5. **She:** Those potato chips are too greasy; they're not good for your heart.

   He: Right again, snuggle buns. And those greasy fingers could accidentally slip on the trigger of my laser crossbow, which would not be very good for *your* heart.

MEN FIX EVERYTHING

When a woman is a little needy or vulnerable, men don't know how to talk. They have to fix the situation. They have to pontificate — as if someone died and made him pontiff! Before a man pontificates, always refer to him as "Your Royal Highness". This appeals to his ego. Then, after you listen to his bullshit, refer to him as "Your Royal Anus", just to put him in his place. Unfortunately, the best solution a man can give a woman is composed of two parts gin and one part vermouth.

....

The best solution a man can give a woman is composed of two parts gin and one part vermouth.

....

Even though a man is a professional bullshitter, the kind of bullshit he throws depends upon his profession, his line of work.

Let's face it. All a man thinks about is his work. He may think *with* his dick, but he thinks *about* his work. While it is true there are times when a man will dick around with his work — there are other times when he is hard at work — on his dick!

HOW A MAN *THINKS* HE IS CHEERING UP A WOMAN

When a woman tells a man she is feeling miserable, she wants him to cradle her in his arms and tell her, "Don't worry, sweetheart, everything is going to be just fine." The last time this happened was in a Spencer Tracy/Katharine Hepburn movie in 1952. The actual scene was cut, however, because the producers felt it was too unrealistic.

Instead, a man will try to "fix" the situation, only he will fix it according to the blinding barrage of bullshit emanating out of "His Eminence's" line of work or profession. For example:

WOMAN: I feel miserable.

MAN: (Nutritionist or Dietician) It's because you haven't been taking your B-complex multi-triglycerides with added bee pollen, blue-green algae and spirulina-protein-packed enzymes. You should also be taking 10 tablespoons of lecithin-flax-seed oil along with 18 gigagrams of calcium-magnesium-bifido-echinacea acidophilus. You also haven't moved your bowels in three days.

WOMAN: I feel miserable.

MAN: (Financial Planner) That's because you are experiencing a low yield due to the fact that you haven't invested a minimum of 30 percent of your portfolio in high-yield growth stocks and 20 per cent in secure, yet high-return mutual funds. In addition, switch the money you have in treasury bills to tax-

free municipal bonds. Also, you maxed out your
MasterCard at Macy's. You're broke, bitch!

WHEN A MAN KEEPS "FIXING YOU",
HOW TO FIX HIM, BUT GOOD!

A woman gets sick and tired of a man's incessant solutions. Let
his crotch bleed seven days a month and see if he's so glib with
his "fix-it" phrases. It's not time to get mad, it's time to get even
(see also the Hate Letter Technique, Chapter 11 and How to
Wage War, Chapter 12).

For the Nutritionist, Dietician: When he's sleeping, shove 1400
gelatin capsules of Mega Power III multi-vitamins up his ass.
When he's in the bathroom the next morning and the toilet
explodes, tell him it's a new colonic you read about in
Prevention magazine.

For the Financial Planner: When he's at work watching other
people's money — *you* go to work watching *his* money. Forge his
signature and put all his assets in your Swiss bank account and
then fly to Rome. Shop 'til you drop using his platinum Visa.
When you return, sue him for neglect because he can't afford to
care for you in the manner to which you will soon become
accustomed.

CHAPTER 3

WOMEN YATTA YATTA
MEN GO TO THE COUCH

Men and women react to stress differently. When a woman is stressed, she likes to talk — either that or she goes to the mall and shops until the little guy on her American Express card has beads of sweat on his forehead. Men, on the other hand, become totally withdrawn and moody. They like to go to the couch and stare at the TV with the glazed eyes of a creature from *The Night of the Living Dead*. They flick the remote endlessly in an attempt to break the Olympic World Record for "shortest attention span by a zombie".

**God forbid a man should put down
the remote and emote!**

Women, on the other hand, need to talk and have an emotional connection with their partner. But nooo...a man needs to zone out on the couch. God forbid a man should put down the remote and emote!

When a woman wants to talk, a man will usually revert to his stock line, "I think I have a brain tumor" to avoid discussion. A man would rather run up and down a basketball court for five straight hours. That's relaxing. Sitting and listening for five minutes — that's exhausting! By learning to listen to a woman's feelings, a man can effectively shower her with the caring, devotion, and understanding she needs. Or he can just take a shower, which in many cases will please her even more.

MEN GO TO THE COUCH

A man goes to the couch for two reasons. The first reason, he needs to allow his problems and issues to gestate for a while, to lie fallow, get better and clearer with time. In other words he needs to fuck off!

A woman doesn't realize the kinds of pressures a man is under; pressures which need lots of time to resolve. A man needs

to figure out whether to stab Bill, the VP of Operations, in the back, or whether to suck up to Ed, the VP of Marketing. He needs to figure out how to tell his wife about the three-year affair he's been having before she hears about it from Bill, the VP of Operations. And, most important, he needs to find $65,000 by next Friday in order to pay the extortion money demanded by Bill, the VP of Operations.

The second reason a man goes to the couch is to drive a woman crazy. Nothing drives a woman more insane than watching her man lie on the couch for hours on end watching the dumbest shows she has ever seen — especially fishing.

A woman will say to herself, "Oh look, Billy Bob is casting off...Wow! Ker-plunk! The lure hit the water. Now Billy Bob will stand in the boat for five hours waiting for something to bite. The excitement is just overwhelming. If Billy Bob actually pulls up a fucking fish, not only will my mascara run from tears of joy, but I'm going to wet my pants from a multiple orgasm."

This technique is very effective at driving a woman to drink or pushing her over the edge, which is why men should use it all the time.

WOMEN YATTA YATTA

When a woman is stressed out, she talks — on and on, yatta, yatta, yatta. When a woman is not stressed out, she also talks on and on. Generally speaking, a woman is generally speaking. Many men are under the misconception that a woman always has to have the last word. This is not true because *a woman never gets to the last word!*

....

Many men are under the misconception that a woman always has to have the last word. This is not true because *a woman never gets to the last word!*

....

Many people ask what do women talk about? But it is more accurate to ask what women do *not* talk about, and that answer is very clear: "tungsten arc welding". Women never talk about tungsten arc welding, though they talk about everything else. If they do talk about tungsten arc welding, however, it is how they *feel* about tungsten arc welding, and who are *cute* tungsten arc welders, but never about tungsten arc welding itself.

A lot of women's talk, however, is gossip, and many a woman has picked up more dirt with her telephone than with her vacuum cleaner. This is not to imply that a woman will repeat gossip — at least not the way she heard it. Nor is it to imply that a woman can't keep a secret, because she will often say, "I'm telling you this in confidence because it was told to *me* in confidence." What we are saying is that if a woman hears something that leaves her speechless — you can be sure she'll talk about it.

....

Many a woman has picked up more dirt with her telephone than with her vacuum cleaner.

....

WHAT MEN ARE *SAYING* WHILE A WOMAN IS TALKING.

You can always count on a man to hold his own in a conversation. These are only a few of the things a man will say if, in fact, he's capable of saying anything at all.

1. Uh Huh.

2. I see.

3. Interesting.

4. Hmmmm...

5. Really?

6. No kidding?

7. Yeah, uh huh.

8. Imagine that.

During this period a man should keep nodding like those toy dogs with the bobbing heads you see in the back of cars.

WHAT MEN ARE *THINKING* WHILE A WOMAN IS TALKING.

Contrary to women's beliefs, however, men's minds are engaged when a woman is talking. This is usually what he is thinking.

1. The last time I saw a mouth like hers there was a fishhook in it.

2. God, can this woman talk up a storm. She must be doing 150 words a minute. With gusts up to 190.

3. I can see why they call this nut cake "Amazon". She's so wide at the mouth.

4. This woman can chew a man's ear off faster than Mike Tyson in a rematch.

5. This bimbo's conversation is riveting. I wonder if her bra clasps in the front or the back?

6. If this bitch keeps up with this yatta yatta, I'm going to handcuff her, frisk her, and tell her she has a right to remain silent. And then I'm going to frisk her again.

HOW A MAN DEALS WITH HIS STRESSFUL DAY

A man does not need the same emotional venting that a woman needs. Here is an example of what Rudy says when he comes home from work:

"Hi honey! I'm home. What a day! I am so stressed! Wanna know why? My boss is an asswipe, I hated the commute, and everybody at my presentation gave me a hard time. Whew! Boy, I feel better now! I love these little talks we have — really takes a load off! Got any cold beer?"

HOW A WOMAN DEALS WITH HER STRESSFUL DAY:

A woman, however, needs a little more time to vent and let the bad air out. For example, Dolores comes home from work exasperated and says:

Hi honey! What a day! I am so stressed! Wanna know why? Well, first of all as you know, the alarm didn't go off on time this morning, and I got up 20 minutes late, which was weird because I was dreaming I was awake — ever do that? Dream you're awake? It's the craziest thing! It seems so real doesn't it? Anyway, I'm dreaming I'm awake and all dressed up for the office, except, instead of a business suit, I'm wearing a wet suit, you know, a skin-diving outfit? And instead of fins, I was wearing bowling shoes, which in my dream looked really hot. Are you listening? Anyway, I go to the kitchen to get some coffee, and who's sitting at the table but Woody Allen! And he's got the coffee all made and he's offering me a toasted bagel with the really good Nova lox and Philadelphia cream cheese spread on it — I guess he would have the good stuff 'cause he is Jewish after all. Anyway, I'm like, "Thanks, Woody, but I'm watching my fat intake." Christ, even in my dreams I'm denying myself. That's not right is it? Anyway, I say I'm watching my fat intake and Woody says, "Y-y-y-ou're beautiful the way you are y-y-y'know, you're a-a polymorphously perfect specimen of femininity and youthful vitality, and not only that — your ass looks good in a wetsuit." You know how he talks in that stuttering way? Now I'm flattered 'cause Woody usually goes for gals a lot younger than me, so I'm thinking what the hell. And besides, I've always loved his movies. So as I reach for the bagel, Woody suddenly turns into Richard Simmons in an evil clown mask! Ahhhh! And before I know it, I'm tied spread-eagle on a huge neon Deal-a-Meal dial, and each time I go around a fat lady in a muumuu slaps me and tells me cream cheese is the devil. What a nightmare! Or morningmare, in this case. Are you listening? Anyway, I wake up in a cold sweat starving! I get dressed and rush to the office. Halfway there I realize it's my turn to open up but I forgot the keys! So I rush back home to get the keys, which takes me 20 minutes to find because I switched bags, and they were in my chartreuse clutch and not in my navy shoulder bag which I originally thought. So I rush back to the office, and on the way over I get a flat. I pull over, put the spare on, and in the process break two nails which I just had done yesterday. I mean *just* had done, like yesterday afternoon! God I hate that! At $2.50 a pop! I don't know how a little bit of acrylic powder and some liquid can be so expensive. Anyway, finally, I make it to the office, open up, rush in, make coffee, get my desk organized, and realize there's nobody there but me. Know why there's nobody there but me? 'CAUSE TODAY'S FUCKING LABOR DAY, THAT'S WHY!

After this spiel and a few moments of silence, the woman feels much better and says to her man, "Ooo, wow! I feel so much better getting it all out! Ahhhhhh, that's such a relief. Wasn't that an incredible story, honey?"

At this point the man prepares his reply by going to the shed for his pick ax, chain saw, and sling blade.

HOW TO TALK TO A WOMAN WITHOUT LISTENING

Very often a woman's chattering is so annoying that she can distract a man from important activities, like reading the sports section, the comic page, or the latest specials on motor oil. Nevertheless, it is important that the woman doesn't realize he's not paying attention. Here are a few ways he can talk to her without listening.

> **When she says,** "You don't Listen."
> **He says,** (reading the paper) "Of course I miss Tim, how is he?"

> **When she says,** "I feel like I'm not that important to you."
> **He says,** (while watching television) "Of course you're important……..Ellen, right?…no, I'm sorry……it's Lisa? Hey, where ya goin' Debbie?"

> **When she says,** "You have no feelings, you're in your head."
> **He says,** (playing a computer game) "I'd feel great if you gave me head!"

HOW A MAN LISTENS, BUT DOESN'T "HEAR"

It's possible a man may listen to the words a woman is saying, but rarely will he understand where she is coming from. For example:

> **She says,** "You're not romantic. You're too intellectual."
> **He says,** "My response to your assessment, in fact, is that you have arrived at an obviously illogical conclusion deduced from an insufficient analysis of the psycho-

emotive qualities of my behavior. In fact, the kinesthetic component of my disposition is surprisingly high when compared to a standard-deviation statistical analysis of the populace at large."

When she says, "You don't care about what happens to me."
He says, "Are you kidding? What about that million-dollar life insurance policy I have on you? Now hurry up or you'll be late for your free-fall sky-diving lesson."

HOW TO MANIPULATE
THE OPPOSITE SEX

Manipulating the opposite sex is crucial to getting even in your relationships. You need to know what buttons to push and how to push them to achieve maximum control and domination.

WHAT MOTIVATES THE SEXES?

Knowing your opponent's motivation is your key to success. To sum it up, women are motivated when they are feeling loved, adored, and cherished. Men are motivated when they are feeling.....a woman!

....

Women are motivated when they are feeling loved, adored, and cherished. Men are motivated when they are feeling.....a woman!

....

Just knowing these simple principles will enable you to have the opposite sex wrapped around your finger in no time. If the techniques fail, you can simply have sex with your finger, which will probably be even more satisfying.

For men this means that flattery will get you everywhere with a woman, unless she happens to be a drill sergeant in the Marines, in which case "yes ma'am/no ma'am" might be as adoring and cherishing as you can get without getting a combat boot in your groin. For women this means that sexual teasing will get you everywhere.

TO MANIPULATE EFFECTIVELY YOU MUST REALIZE YOU ARE NOT DEALING WITH A PERSON, YOU ARE DEALING WITH AN OBJECT

For Women, Men are Success Objects

A woman likes to be with a man who has something on the ball — even better, something on the NASDAQ. This is why a woman often falls in love at second sight. The first time she didn't know he was rich.

When a woman falls in love with a man, she will start feeling sexy, often using baby language like "sweetie pie", "honey-poo", and "snuggly dumpling". But, once he is off guard, she will begin using adult language like "charge account", "mortgage payment", and "car insurance". She'll then look to her man to say those four magic words: "Here's my credit card". As a matter of fact, she'll believe in giving her man all the credit she can get.

....

A woman often falls in love at second sight.
The first time she didn't know he was rich.

....

Remember, at first a woman may be attracted to a certain bulge, but keep in mind — the real bulge she wants is in a guy's wallet. No woman likes going out with some cheap-ass that wants to take her on a date "Dutch Treat". Where's the treat there? She orders the jerk chicken, next thing you know, the jerk she's with is asking her to pay half, and she's having an out-of-wallet experience! Men need to know that a woman's slogan is, "Pay all, or get none!"

For Men, Women Are Sex Objects

For men, women are sex objects. Some people may argue this is a superficial way to think. It's a known fact, however, that superficiality is highly underrated. Men want sex. No man is ever going to nudge his buddy and say, "Hey, check out the mind on that chick over there! What a cranium!" Men aren't into craniums, they're into *cups*, preferably C and D cups.

....

For men, women are sex objects. Some people may
argue this is a superficial way to think. It's a known fact,
however, that superficiality is highly underrated.

....

Men prefer that women have as little on their minds as they have on their bodies.

Dressing for Succ-Sex

Remember that a woman must turn a man on if she's going to do a man in. So it doesn't matter if a woman is vague on the inside, she should be *vogue* on the outside. Less-dressed is better than best-dressed, and a woman just can't wear too much of not enough.

....

Less-dressed is better than best-dressed, and a woman just can't wear too much of not enough.

....

RELATIONSHIPS ARE A MATTER OF GIVE AND TAKE

Experts agree that relationships should be a harmonious dance of give and take. After a woman gives in to the urges of a man, she should take him for all he's worth. Remember that ladies who give a man his share of sex will end up with their own shares of Microsoft.

....

Ladies who give a man his share of sex will end up with their own shares of Microsoft.

....

HOW TO FLATTER THE PANTS OFF A WOMAN

Although men are "flatulence-propelled", women are "flattery-operated". Women love to be flattered. But the man must know the correct way to flatter in order to achieve his goal, which is

WOMEN ARE FLATTERY OPERATED

complete and total submission. Achieving this illustrious, low-life goal takes a bit of time, and a man must start off slow, building the flattery to a fine-tuned crescendo.

To do this a man must understand a woman's needs, which are simple and constant. Women need to:

1. Feel young

2. Feel skinny

3. Feel sexy

A man must make reference to these needs under all circumstances, at every possible opportunity. For example, he might say:

(Her need to feel young)

"When the beam of the officer's flashlight hit your panic-stricken face after he stopped you for speeding, I couldn't help but think how you looked sixteen years old again — just like the first time you were arrested for shoplifting."

(Her need to feel skinny)

"Gee, I'm real sorry your grandfather died, but as you were leaning over the coffin to kiss him goodbye, I noticed how slim your ass looked."

(Her need to feel sexy)

"You know, when those baggy sweatpants cling to your buttocks as you lumber to the fridge for yet another Dove Bar, I just go wild! I don't know whether to grab you by your expandable-elastic waistband, or wrestle you to the ground in a pagan fertility ritual."

Notice how a man can use these seemingly inappropriate situations as an opportunity for flattery. Before you know it, by using these simple methods, you'll have a woman so flattered, she'll be flat on her back!

HOW TO GET A MAN TO DO WHAT YOU WANT

Women are under the illusion that they don't have to ask men for anything — that if the man really loved her, he would automatically and instinctively know what she needed. Right! As if the dysfunctional drone even knew she was in the room, let alone knew what she was feeling. A woman has a better chance of finding a bathing suit off the rack that fits than finding a man who knows what she is going through.

Ironically, however, men like to feel needed — like they're her knight in shining armor. Unfortunately, most turn out to be needy, like her nightmare from *The Shining*. Therefore, it is important that a woman ask a man directly for what she wants, not indirectly. He is not a mind reader. He doesn't even read a map, how's he going to read a mind?

....

A woman has a better chance of finding a bathing suit off the rack that fits than finding a man who knows what she is going through.

....

HOW TO ASK A MAN TO DO SOMETHING

Always remember these five important rules when asking a man to do something:

1. Make sure the man is conscious.

2. Crash the hard drive on his computer and line the bird cage with the sports section.

3. Be brief! Limit your nagging harangue to two, three hours, max.

4. Reward him for cooperative behavior. Offer to cook him something that doesn't have a peel-back cover.

5. Punish him when he refuses to cooperate. Microwave his remote on high power for 55 minutes. Rotate 1/4 turn, and microwave again for another 35 minutes.

6. Use "would you" or "will you" instead of "you'd better" or "do as I say and no one will get hurt".

OK, six rules.

THE RIGHT AND WRONG WAY TO ASK A MAN

How you ask a man to do something makes all the difference. Women think that a subtle nuance or a slight turn of the phrase will have no effect whatsoever on the resolve of their indomitable pumped-up mucho-macho muscular moron. It does! Which is why you should always use "would you" and "will you" instead of "could you" and "can you". For example:

Do say: *would* you take out the garbage?
Do not say: *could* you get off your fat ass and do something around here? What am I, the fucking maid?

Do say: *would* you like to have a ménage-a-trois with our next-door-neighbor, Betty?
Do not say: *could* you learn how to perform oral sex on me so I don't have to have a lesbian affair with our next-door-neighbor, Betty?

Do say: *would* you like to go out to a nice dinner Saturday night?
Do not say: *could* you please take me to any restaurant that doesn't have the words "burger", "king", or "happy meal" in their advertising?

Do say: *would* you mind watching the kids while I take a night off with my girlfriends?
Do not say: *could* you, just for one night, watch the kids you helped spawn — that I never get a break from — *ever?* I haven't seen my friends in so long we wear name tags to identify ourselves.

Do say: *would* you take me to a movie this week?
Do not say: *could* you prove you're not Velcroed to the couch and actually have the motor skills to take me to a motion picture? Something without Pamela Anderson in it.

Do say: *would* you like me to listen to you talk about your day some more?
Do not say: *could* you step up the filibuster, Sparky? *Jeopardy* is on in ten minutes.

Do say: *would* you consider getting a vasectomy?
Do not say: *could* you even imagine what it feels like taking birth control pills that make you feel like Attila the Hun one minute and Attila the Hun's evil twin the next minute? No? Then get your tubes tied or I'll have your dick snipped.

Do say: *would* you like to take a vacation?
Do not say: *could* you move out?

Do say: *would* you get out of my life?
Do not say: *could* you get out of my life?

Notice how different these two statements are. A man is much more likely to get out of your life if you say "would".

HOW TO MOTIVATE A MAN BY BECOMING A DOMINATRIX

Big rough-and-tumble men in high-powered positions often have a side that most people don't see. While publicly they like to boss everyone around, privately they like to be put in a leather mask, a choke collar, and told to "heel".

The following are commands and techniques that will make a man your obedient slave:

1.   Dress him in a dog collar with a leash. Strap soapy sponges to his hands and knees and make him scrub the kitchen floor while singing, "I'm Forever Blowing Bubbles".

2.   Whip him into giving you a pedicure while you browse the new *Spiegel* catalog.

3. After dressing him in a French maid's outfit, chain him to your Maytag and, before doing the laundry, force him to separate the whites from the colors.

4. Dress him in a chauffeur's uniform and handcuff him to the steering wheel. Demand that he learn the shortcuts to every shopping mall within a 50-mile radius.

5. Using an electric cattle prod, condition him to say key phrases on command like, "You're looking thinner and sexier every day", "Other women? What other women?", and the ultimate, "What can I do to make myself worthy of you, Oh Grand-Exalted-Mistress-Of-The-Universe?"

Reward good behavior with treats. Lite-beer enemas go over very well.

CHAPTER 5
THE FINE ART OF
MISCOMMUNICATION

While a lot of people talk about communication, trust us, it's all talk. No communication actually takes place. What in fact takes place is *miscommunication*. And to survive and get even in your relationships, you need to learn the fine art of miscommunication.

You see in the beginning it was common knowledge that Brassierians and Penusians spoke different tongues. They even used different hand gestures, although when they gave each other the finger, everyone knew what it meant.

But they got along well, even though they spoke different languages. If they had a problem, they would go to a translator. These translators were usually union and demanded time-and-a-half. As the overtime mounted, however, they wrote the Brassierian-to-Penusian and Penusian-to-Brassierian Dictionary to decipher the difference between what was said versus what was actually meant.

THE BRASSIERIAN TO PENUSIAN PHRASE DICTIONARY

When she says: Take me to a nice restaurant.
Translated means: I want to go somewhere where a shirt is required and the entree doesn't pop out of a vending machine when you press B5.

When she says: Everyone ignores me.
Translated means: If you don't pay attention to me, I'm going to have an illicit affair with the Dallas Cowboys — and all their cheerleaders!

When she says: Me, jealous? Ha!
Translated means: If you so much as look at another woman, I will have you spayed and neutered.

When she says: I found the greatest sale today!
Translated means: I bought five times as much.

When she says: I love your family.
Translated means: On another continent.

When she says: It doesn't take a lot of money to make me happy.
Translated means: But let's start with all you've got.

When she says: My girlfriend just got engaged.
Translated means: My ring better be on its way, buster.

When she says: You don't understand PMS!
Translated means: *I* don't understand PMS.

When she says: I think I love you.
Translated means: I haven't thought about a divorce
                          for nearly three hours and eleven
                          minutes.

When she says: Do you think that woman is
                          attractive?
Translated means: You'd better say no.

When she says: If I see your face glued to that
                          fucking TV set one more minute
                          — I'm going to shove the remote
                          up your ass!
Translated means: If I see your face glued to that
                          fucking TV set one more minute
                          — I'm going to shove the remote
                          up your ass!

THE PENUSIAN TO BRASSIERIAN PHRASE DICTIONARY

When he says: No, those jeans don't make you look fat.

Translated means: It's all those extra cookies, pies and cakes you ate that make you look fat.

When he says: I hate Valentine's Day. They gouge you for cards, candy, and flowers.

Translated means: I'm a cheapskate.

When he says: I'm in the exact same shape as when I was 21.

Translated means: Even then I got out of breath playing chess.

When he says: It's guy stuff.

Translated means: There's chips, beer, and porno movies involved.

When he says: I'm not lost. I know where I'm going!

Translated means: Right now even Rand-McNally would be sending up flares.

When he says: Uggh! That's a chick movie.

Translated means: It's sensitive with a real plot, real characters, and Bruce Willis isn't getting blown up.

When he says: You're the only one for me.

Translated means: You're the only one who puts up with my shit.

When he says:	You're a highly skilled woman.
Translated means:	You can bait a hook.
When he says:	I love you just the way you are.
Translated means:	The mortician who did your make-up made you look almost lifelike.
When he says:	I find you fascinating!
Translated means:	You actually listen to me!
When he says:	I don't understand what you're saying.
Translated means:	I know you're right. I just don't want to admit it.

With regular and persistent use you will soon see why the *Penusian-To-Brassierian Dictionary* is absolutely and totally useless.

....

All a woman is ever *really* saying is, "I'm feeling vulnerable and I need a hug." While all a man ever *really* says is nothing, nothing at all. Translated that means, "I'm feeling vulnerable, so leave me the fuck alone!"

....

In the first place, all a woman is ever *really* saying is, "I'm feeling vulnerable and I need a hug." While all a man ever *really* says is nothing, nothing at all. Translated that means, "I'm feeling vulnerable, so leave me the fuck alone!"

6

MEN GO UP AND DOWN
LIKE YO-YO'S

Women will be better able to deal with men if they understand the pattern of men's behavior. Men are like yo-yos. They go up and down, up and down — and never at the right time. Just when a woman wants a man to be up — he droops down. Just when she wants him to be down — something pops up — usually at 6AM when she's fast asleep.

....

Just when a woman wants a man to be up — he droops down. Just when she wants him to be down — something pops up — usually at 6AM when she's fast asleep.

....

This pattern can be very confusing to a woman. When a man pulls away at the wrong time, a woman may ask herself:

- Is it because my arm fat jiggles?

- Should I get my roots done?

- Who needs this shit?

The thing a woman must remember is a man is a yo-yo. He goes up and down, in and out. He alternates between needing intimacy, needing autonomy, and needing money. Therefore, sometimes a man needs to pull away completely — before he finally leaves for good.

....

Sometimes a man needs to pull away completely — before he finally leaves for good.

....

A woman doesn't realize that in intimacy a man loses himself through connecting with his partner, which is why, after he pulls away, she should tell him to get lost!

A woman though, being a woman, will want to *talk* to him about what's bothering him. Talking to a man, however, takes enormous skill and patience. You can't just talk to him at any time. There are *conditions*.

MAN PLAYING WITH HIS YO-YO

WHEN TO TALK TO A MAN

There are definitely right and wrong times for a woman to talk to a man. If she wants something in return — like a response. First of all, a man needs to be in the *mood* to talk. He can't just *talk*. Everything has to be right. The temperature has to be cool, generally around 69°, the humidity has to be balmy, about 50% or lower, the wind should be gentle, no more than 10 miles per hour, with the barometric pressure 30.1 and rising. In addition, there are other factors that could contribute to your successful attempt at communicating:

1. He should have a pulse.

2. He should be someone you know.

3. He should recognize you without asking for I.D..

4. He should be in the same room — or at least the same country.

5. He should be fluent in your language — or carry a pocket phrase dictionary.

6. In his head he should not be listening to dead people talking.

7. He should have taken his medication.

8. He should have no outstanding warrants for his arrest.

The Worst Times To Talk To A Man

• When he's being arraigned in court.

• When he's on "the throne" after eating a bowl of Mexican chili.

• When he's about to go for a birdie on the 9th hole and the windmill keeps getting in the way.

• When he's on a date with someone else.

The Best Times To Talk To A Man

- When he's finally finished that 4-inch-high bird house that cost him $1,200 in power tools to construct.

- When the guy at the office, who was in competition with him for the big promotion, gets caught in the men's room wearing ladies' underwear.

- Right after you promise him oral sex.

WHEN MEN DON'T TALK

When a man is silent, his silence can be very threatening to a woman, and all she may feel like doing is slapping the shit out of him to elicit some kind of response. She asks, "What's wrong?" He finally says, "I need my space."

She's thinking, "Then become a fucking astronaut!"

A man will lay on the couch for hours, a silent lone potato, but a woman will still try to get her man to talk. She doesn't realize she is interrupting his internal process of figuring out the terribly important problem that is plaguing him, which is, "I wonder if the Yankees will win the Series again this year?"

By understanding the man's need be silent, a woman can better understand a man's need to get even by providing behavior that is annoying, irritating, stupid, illogical, self-serving, self-absorbed, unreasonable, incomprehensible, reprehensible, cold, and insensitive. Which is what attracted her to him in the first place.

HOW WOMEN REACT TO THE SILENCE

How does a woman react when a man is silent? In a word, *not good.* That's actually two words, but believe it, nothing makes her feel more insecure. She starts playing the Catastrophe Channel in her head: "He's rejecting me! It's my thighs. I should never have eaten that 11th package of Twinkies. He is leaving me forever!"

....

He is not leaving you. If a man doesn't have the energy to get off the couch, how is he going to have the energy to pack?

....

No such luck. Relax. He is not leaving you. If a man doesn't have the energy to get off the couch, how is he going to have the energy to pack?

WHEN A MAN WON'T TALK: THE ONE-SIDED CONVERSATION

Nothing drives a woman crazier than when she tries to talk to a guy and he answers her with that glazed, self-absorbed look on his face. A one-sided conversation may go like this:

DIANNE: How was your day?

BEN: Okay.

DIANNE: How did that meeting go with your boss?

BEN: Okay.

DIANNE: I got your clothes back from the cleaners today.

BEN: Okay.

DIANNE: Want to do something tonight?

BEN: Okay.

DIANNE: Shall I come up with a suggestion?

BEN: Okay.

DIANNE: (getting annoyed) OKAY? OKAY, then I'm going to invite Missy's old boyfriend, Brad, over. Missy tells me he has a 10-inch penis and a body like an Adonis. I think I'll fly with him to the Virgin Islands for a two-week affair at a four-star hotel, book the honeymoon suite with a heart-shaped Jacuzzi, a rotating mirrored bed, and order champagne and caviar from room service, and have sex, sex, sex 'round the clock — in every position imaginable! SO WHAT DO YOU THINK ABOUT THAT? IS THAT OKAY????

BEN: That's awful! You know you're allergic to caviar.

HOW TO GET A MAN TO TALK

To get a man to talk is relatively easy, once you know how. The following are a few basic rules that are crucial to your success:

First, have him repeat simple two-syllable words like, "ma-ma", "da-da", and "you're thin".

Then, teach him how to respond to simple commands like, "sit", "stay", "roll over", and "pick up the check".

Finally, shift the conversation from things *he* is interested in to things *you* are interested in. For example, if you're watching a football game, say, "Wasn't that a great play by the half-back? And speaking of 'half-back', they had a 50% off sale at Bloomingdale's where I found this beautiful dress that gives me a really tight end which I scored with your credit card."

HOW TO STOP A WOMAN FROM TALKING

Obviously, the only way to stop a woman from talking is to put something in her mouth.

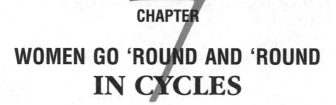

CHAPTER

WOMEN GO 'ROUND AND 'ROUND
IN CYCLES

A woman's emotions go 'round in cycles. 'Round and 'round she goes, where she stops, nobody knows — especially her! Frankly, she doesn't have a "bloody" clue!

This, of course, drives a man absolutely nuts! How is a man supposed to understand a woman's cycle, when he can't even understand a rinse cycle?

....

How is a man supposed to understand a woman's cycle, when he can't even understand a rinse cycle?

....

THE POSITIVE CYCLE

A woman's monthly cycle has two parts, positive and negative. During the positive part of the cycle, a woman is happy, carefree, bouncy — all smiles. She is a cross between the Easter Bunny and a used-car salesman meeting you for the first time. This is when a woman gets her *exclamation point!*

THE NEGATIVE CYCLE

The negative part of the cycle is a little different. When a woman is going through her negative cycle, S.W.A.T. teams call in sick, the Joint Chiefs at the Pentagon wave the white flag to surrender, and Godzilla runs for cover!

Needless to say, it's bad, very bad. This is when a woman gets her *period*, because she is completely and totally miserable — **PERIOD!**

SURVIVING A WOMAN'S CYCLE

What can a man do to work with a woman's cycles? The answer is very simple. NOTHING! Not a goddamn thing! The only hope a man has in working with a woman's cycle is knowing when a woman is in her positive cycle and when she's in her negative cycle so he can adjust his behavior accordingly.

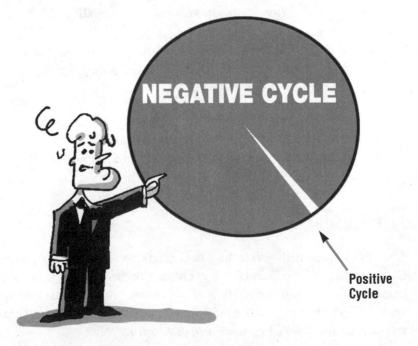

Positive
Cycle

Of course this presents a problem, because of the 28 days, a woman is in her positive cycle for exactly 3 hours, 29 minutes, and 13 seconds. THE REST OF THE TIME SHE IS IN HER NEGATIVE CYCLE! If a man happens to be tuning his carburetor, oiling his chain saw, or farting in the john, HE MISSES THE ENTIRE POSITIVE CYCLE! He may never even know that it occurred — let alone what hit him.

....

If a man happens to be tuning his carburetor, oiling his chain saw, or farting in the john, HE MISSES THE ENTIRE POSITIVE CYCLE!

....

There may be 5 minutes when a woman is a little "frisky" and he can score. But if he misses those 5 minutes, he will have to walk like Quasimodo for another 28 days until hc can get laid.

HOW A MAN CAN TELL IF A WOMAN IS GETTING HER PERIOD

Knowing when a woman is getting her period is important because this could be the perfect time to write your will and notify your next-of-kin. A few indications are:

1. She stops reading *Glamour* and starts reading *Guns and Ammo*.

2. She considers chocolate a major FDA food group.

3. You ask her what time it is, and she replies, "What do you mean I look fat?!"

4. She makes you sleep on the couch because all the potato chips and cheese doodles have taken up your side of the bed.

WOMAN IN HER NEGATIVE CYCLE

5. She puts on one of those pads with "wings", then flies off the roof laughing hysterically.

6. Her jeans grow 2 sizes larger while her canine teeth grow 2 inches longer.

7. She's developed a new talent for spinning her head around in 360° circles.

8. She retains more water than Lake Superior.

9. She denies she's in a bad mood as she pops a clip into her semi-automatic and "chambers one".

10. She buys you a new T-shirt — with a bulls-eye on the front.

11.   You ask her to please pass the salt at the dinner table and she says, "All I ever do is give, give, give! AM I SUPPOSED TO DO EVERYTHING?"

12.   She answers every question with the same answer, "Over my dead body!"

13.   She's more paranoid than O.J. Simpson in a Bruno Magli shoe store.

14.   She looks at you through her thumb and index finger and makes the "I'll squish your tiny head" gesture.

15.   She enrolls in the Lizzie Borden School of Charm.

16.   She orders 3 Big Macs, 4 large fries, a bucket of Chicken McNuggets, and then mauls the manager because they're out of Diet Coke.

During this negative cycle a man may very gently and sensitively say, "Pardon me, honey, I hope I am not in any way showing that I don't cherish you as much as I cherish my own yo-yo, but did you ever get your exclamation point this month? Did you perhaps feel somewhat pleasant for a few minutes? Think. Think hard."

These type of sarcastic, snot-nose remarks are good because she will get so angry and upset she will completely forget about her negative cycle.

When a woman forgets about her negative cycle, she will enter into one of two conditions. If she is in a state of *low energy*, she sinks down into the pits. If she is in a state of *high energy*, she will enter into a state which we call WAR! *(see Chapter 12, How To Wage War)*.

WHEN A WOMAN SINKS INTO THE PITS

When a woman sinks down into the pits, any depressing emotion will rise to the surface. Whether the emotion originated when

Billy Jo Snitbottom snapped her bra in seventh grade or when her sixth husband became a transsexual and had an affair with himself, you can be sure that the skeletons of the past will come rushing out of the closet.

All her *back issues* will start to surface. She'll say stuff like, "I was looking for this issue of *Cosmo* from 1985. And I found it — right under the butcher knives and ice pick where I left it. It's got my favorite article in it: 'How to Use and Abuse Men, Yet Still Appear Coy and Childlike.'"

A man supporting a woman when she is in the pits is a special gift that she will greatly appreciate — not as much as a Porsche, a diamond tennis bracelet, or oral sex for an hour, but it's better than nothing.

Tell-Tale Signs She May Be Sinking Into The Pits

Here are some definite hints that a woman may be sinking into the pits:

She feels	She may say
Insecure	The Michelin man has thighs smaller than mine!
Demanding	I wanted two quarts of Rocky Road, you idiot — not Double Mocha Chip! Now drive back in this blizzard and get it!
Suspicious	*Good morning??* Just how am I supposed to take that?
Disapproving	You're wearing that? What're you the cover boy for *Clown Wear Daily*?

She feels	She may say
Passive	I don't care what you wear. I'm used to the guilt and shame of being in your company.
Exhausted	Do you think I like bitching non-stop for hours at a time? It's very tiring pointing out all your glaring faults!
Hopeless	Just get me a Dr. Kevorkian gift certificate.

When a woman sinks into the pits, this is when she needs the unconditional love and support of a man. A real man, not the jerk farting on the couch reading *Fishing Lure Weekly.*

....

When a woman sinks into the pits, this is when she needs the unconditional love and support of a man. A real man, not the jerk farting on the couch reading *Fishing Lure Weekly.*

....

HOW A MAN CAN SUPPORT A WOMAN WHILE SHE'S IN THE PITS

When a woman is in the pits, it is important that a man not try to fix the situation. Instead, he should listen with caring, warmth, and empathy. Then let the bitch drown! It's important that she wallow in the mud for a while. Let her steep in her own juices. She made her bed, now let her sleep in it. Tell her to put *that* in her pipe and smoke it.

Pretty soon a man should stop saying all these clichés because he's sounding like a real idiot and she "won't want to touch him with a ten-foot pole", "even if he were the last man on earth."

After a woman sinks into the pits, however, she will come back to the surface feeling happy and refreshed. As she breaks out of her negative condition, she is in a state of high energy. This is a perfect time to start an argument (see Chapter 9) or wage a war (see Chapter 12).

CHAPTER 8

DISCOVERING OUR
EMOTIONAL NEEDINESS

Men and women don't know how to satisfy each other's emotional needs. This is because they do not realize that the needs of each other are different. And they don't realize that they don't realize that. They also don't realize that each one is trying to *give* the way they would like to *receive*. Naturally, they don't realize that either! THIS IS CALLED TRUE LOVE BECAUSE NO ONE KNOWS WHAT THE FUCK ANYONE IS DOING!

....

**Since men and women *give* the way they would
like to *receive*, the very best thing is for each
sex to please themselves.**

....

There is a solution to this dilemma. Since men and women *give* the way they would like to *receive*, the very best thing is for each sex to please themselves. This way each gets exactly what they want. If the man or woman is still not happy, they only have themselves to blame.

REACH OUT AND TOUCH YOURSELF

Obviously, the best way to be satisfied is to do everything yourself. If this prospect is not appealing, keep looking at a photograph of your right hand and very soon you'll start to get excited. Don't worry, you can always sue yourself for sexual harassment if things don't work out.

For Men

Since only you know the voodoo that you do, do the voodoo on you, instead of making doo doo on you-know-who.

What this means is sometimes men need to do their voodoo with their yo-yo (while ballerinas need to do their voodoo in a tutu).

That's right tiger, you know what you're looking for — so go after yourself! Be coy with yourself. Play hard to get. Lead yourself on. Play "negative take-away". Tease yourself. After all, you finally have some time to spend with that handsome, dashing hunk known as you. But where should you take you? What should you and you do? Below are some manly suggestions that *you* can enjoy all by yourself.

Option One: Spend an evening on the couch watching nothing but sports — in your boxer shorts. Unshaven. Unbathed. Flatulate freely, then sniff the air. Give yourself the "thumbs up" sign and remark, "Good one!"

Option Two: Stand in the middle of your uncut lawn wearing only your jock strap. Look at your grass and yell at the top of your lungs: "Nag all you want, bitch, I'm not cutting this goddamn lawn. I hope it grows 9 feet high and turns into Viet Nam! Screw it. If it pisses you off, I'll Napalm the fucking lawn! I don't care! All I know is the only thing I'm cutting today is a 16-inch pizza and maybe a few beer farts!" Then quickly run in the house before the cops book you for disturbing the peace and indecent exposure.

Option Three: Visit the automotive department at Sears. Kick some tires. Mumble about the different kinds of steel-belted radials. Breathe in that awesome rubber smell. Run your fingers over the different brands of synthetic car mats. Marvel over cup holders that actually adjust to the size of your cup. Try not to let anyone see you just had an orgasm.

Option Four: Go to your favorite restaurant. What the hell — splurge! Get that extra helping of McNuggets! Order a trough of ketchup and throw in a few fries. So what! No one's around to nag you about fat grams and clogged heart valves. Wash it all down with a fist full of M&M's and a liter of Yoo-Hoo. Belch out the words to "99 Bottles of Beer" as you drive home.

For Women

You finally have some time to spend with that wonderful, brilliant person known as *you*. But where should you take you? What should you and you do? Below are some nifty suggestions. Just remember, never ask yourself out for Saturday night after Wednesday.

Option One: Buy yourself roses — the kind from the florist, not the kind you get from the gnarly cretin in the middle of traffic, and charge them to his credit card. Add to that a good bottle of wine, maybe a *Chateau Verí Expensivé,* then read *Playgirl* for the pictures.

Option Two: Make a lovely dinner for you and your vibrator. Set the little fellow up across the table from you with his own little

plate (he doesn't eat much — not like the human garbage disposal you date). Smile coquettishly at him, and every so often ask, "Are you having a good time, Buzz?"

Option Three: Draw a bubble bath (use oil paints or pastels). And then actually fill a bathtub with water. While you soak, read a meaningful book, something like *Around the World in 80 Malls, The Complete Guide to Writing Checks,* or *101 Nude Photos of Brad Pitt.*

Option Four: Take yourself out dancing. When you get to the club, ask yourself to dance, then giggle and say, "No thanks, I'm with me." Ask yourself again. This time say, "Okay, but no slow dancing." After a few fast numbers, get bold — ask yourself again to slow dance. This time accept. Then grab your own breast and sigh meaningfully. Tell yourself out loud, "I am the only one for me!" Then giggle again as the manager escorts you out.

TWELVE KINDS OF NEEDINESS: WHY SHE NEEDS HIM AND WHY HE NEEDS HER

There are several kinds of valid reasons why a woman needs a man. Men and women each have their own unique, unreasonable, albeit sick parasitic reasons for needing each other. And as we have discovered, people — people who need people — are the sickest, codependent people in the world. Unlike the twelve steps listed in recovery programs, these twelve kinds of neediness have never been recovered from.

....

People — people who need people — are the sickest, codependent people in the world.

....

12 Reasons Why She Needs Him

1. To have someone to check out a noise in the middle of the night.
    Why should she risk her life if there's a crazed maniac in the living room with a pick ax?

2. To have someone to do the barbecuing.
    Why should she risk blowing off her head in case the gas grill explodes?

3. To have someone to put up the Christmas tree.
    Why should she risk having the thing fall over and spear her in the head?

4. To have someone to carry heavy objects.
    Why should she risk tearing the stitches from her new implants?

5. To have someone to take to a wedding.
    Why should she look stupid standing alone at the alter?

6.   To have someone to have sex with.
     Why should she be the major stockholder in Eveready?

7.   To have someone to blame.
     Why should she act like a mature responsible adult?

8.   To have someone else to nag and make miserable.
     Why should she be the only one mired in her own distorted reality?

9.   To have someone to go places with.
     Why should she be the only one visiting the therapist?

10. To have someone to share things with.
     Why should she be the only one paying the mortgage and electric bill?

11. To have someone to love.
     Why should she be the only one touching herself?

12. To have someone to take out the garbage.
     Why should she be the one driving his friends home after the game?

12 Reasons Why He Needs Her

1.   To be there in a crisis.
     He needs her to make more nachos when the game goes into double overtime.

2.   To have a steady sex partner.
     He needs something that doesn't deflate.

3.   To assist him with his grooming habits.
     He needs her to tell him if he has something hanging out of his nose.

4.   To have someone to bring to special occasions.
     Like when he gets a bowling trophy, or is elected Grand Poobah.

5. To be an equal partner.
    He needs her to balance out the weight in the car so the tires don't wear out unevenly.

6. To help him make decisions.
    Visa, MasterCard or American Express.

7. To have someone to confide in.
    Particularly when his name used to be "Lisa" before the operation.

8. To have someone to keep his life active.
    Or at least his bank account active.

9. To have someone he can count on.
    To bail him out of jail.

10. To have someone to share his life with.
    Since none of his friends can stand him anymore.

11. To have someone with whom he can raise a family.
    His divorced sister and five kids need a place to stay.

12. To have someone he can live with and make happy.
    Now that at age 48 he no longer lives with his mother.

THE TWO KINDS OF MEN

There are two kinds of men; one is incredibly defensive and stubborn; the other kind is incredibly stubborn and defensive. Women need to know how to deal with both kinds of men. The way to deal with them is to never try and change them or improve them. As a matter of fact, have nothing to do with them. Don't give them criticism or advice. Don't even give them the time of day.

....

There are two kinds of men; one is incredibly defensive and stubborn; the other kind is incredibly stubborn and defensive.

....

MONEY DOESN'T FULFILL EMOTIONAL NEEDS — UNLESS YOU HAVE AN EMOTIONAL NEED FOR MONEY

"Money is the root of all evil." This statement is usually made by people who don't have any. It's a lot easier to be spiritual and esoteric when you have your own yacht and a vacation home in Palm Springs. Let's face it, you never see a Rolls Royce with a "Shit Happens" bumper sticker on it.

....

Let's face it, you never see a Rolls Royce with a "Shit Happens" bumper sticker on it.

....

Still, many people think money is the root of all evil. Actually, no money is. This is not *entirely* true. In truth, a relationship is better when the couple is filled with love, rather than money. This is why a woman will sue a man for all he's worth in the hopes that if he declares bankruptcy, it will rekindle the magical spark of love that blossomed into the full-blown hate they share today.

CHAPTER 9
HOW TO PROVOKE ARGUMENTS

Arguing is an important part of relationships since it is based on mutual likes and dislikes, namely that a man and woman like to fight, yet they both dislike each other. While the process begins when they are both mad *about* each other, it always ends when they discover they are really mad *at* each other.

....

Arguing is an important part of relationships since it is based on mutual likes and dislikes, namely that a man and woman like to fight, yet they both dislike each other.

....

WHY MEN AND WOMEN ARGUE

Men and women argue for different reasons. For instance, a man argues because he knows he is right, while a woman argues because she knows he is wrong.

....

A man argues because he knows he is right, while a woman argues because she knows he is wrong.

....

Many relationships suffer because of arguments. This is because most people don't have enough of them.

WHY ARGUMENTS ARE GOOD

Arguments are not only good, they are often necessary for a half-embittered, half-disillusioned, half-over relationship to flourish. Some of the reasons arguments are encouraged are as follows:

1. **Arguments show that the other person is actually making some form of contact.**
    Even if he is calling from a pay phone in Guadalajara, disguising his voice as Darth Vader, with his mouth covered with Saran Wrap, Hey! At least he called! At least he was thoughtful enough to make contact. This way she doesn't have to call Robert Stack and try to locate him through *Unsolved Mysteries.*

2. **Arguments allow the release of pent-up feelings.**
    Without arguments too much is held in, bottled up, left to fester, allowed to rot and decay, turn into deep, deep pits of ca ca and doo doo. Arguments, however, allow the release of emotions such as sadness, disappointment, and concern. They release disgust and venom. The ensuing harangues maim and debilitate, launching vicious, merciless salvos on closet-covered wounds, go-for-the-jugular threats of eternal misery, life-long suffering, and excruciating agony and despair. On the other hand arguments can arouse feelings that are a bit un-comfortable, so they need to be handled with discretion.

3. **Arguments get you out of doing unpleasant chores.**
    If you don't like what your partner is asking you to do,
    pick an argument. Then slam the door and walk out.
    You'll be free of doing the unpleasant task and later
    you'll have the perfect excuse for not doing it — you
    were arguing at the time!

4. **Arguments allow the real truth to come out.**
    Without truth and honesty resentment grows, breeding
    bitterness and spite. Then eventually hatred and loathing
    mount until you turn into Mr. or Ms. Hyde. And then,
    one night, when the moon is full...YOU TURN INTO
    YOUR PARENTS! Therefore, you owe it to your
    insignificant other to let them know what a selfish, self-
    centered, invasive, psychotic, narrow-minded bigot they
    are. Point out the endless inane comments they make
    and the asinine way they act in public. Remind them tree
    sloths have better manners. And don't stop at them
    personally. Denounce the Neanderthal family that
    spawned them. Enthusiastically point out their genetic
    deficiencies and lack of social graces. All of this will pave
    the way for the sensitive release of much deeper issues.

5. **Arguments set the stage for great sex.**
    There's nothing like a really good fight to get the sexual
    juices flowing. Angry sex takes the ho-hum out of your
    romantic life. The more you argue and the angrier you
    get, the longer and better the sex will be. Shoot for an
    hour of bashing and put-downs. Never miss an
    opportunity to rehash an old argument. Exhume dead
    issues. Above all, *always* be sure to include the phrase,
    "If it weren't for you, I could have..." (married so and so,
    become a millionaire, been somebody, etc., etc. See
    Chapter 12, How To Blame Your Partner For Everything).
    In no time flat you'll be doing the horizontal boogaloo
    'til your eyes cross.

HOW TO COMMUNICATE THAT YOU ARE HAVING AN ARGUMENT

It is always good to know if your partner is arguing. This way you can act appropriately and exhibit behavior you would not have otherwise had you not realized the other person was, in fact, arguing. Once you realize the other person is arguing, you should choose between fight or flight.

Fight is getting into combat fatigues and hunkering down for a bitter war of attrition. When you choose **flight** you simply allow the other person to keep arguing while you take off for a skiing trip to Vermont. Then, when you return from the trip, you will find not only that the other person is still arguing, in most cases, they never realized you were gone.

By reading the other person's facial expressions and body language and listening carefully to subtle, tell-tale clues, it is possible to actually detect whether one of the two of you are arguing.

HOW TO TELL IF YOU'RE HAVING AN ARGUMENT

1. If one of you is speaking in Albuquerque and the windows shatter in the World Trade Center, *chances are you're having an argument.*

2. If she pulls out an FBI crime lab report that states that fibers of his secretary's panties were lodged in the bristles of his toothbrush, *chances are you're having an argument.*

3. If she replays the tapes of her previous three 911 calls, *chances are you're having an argument.*

4. If she refers to you as a doll — a voodoo doll, *chances are you're having an argument.*

5. If he rebuts every remark by sticking up his middle finger, *chances are you're having an argument.*

6. You ask her to please pass the hot coffee, and she passes it — all over your groin, *chances are you're having an argument.*

7. If the locks on the house have been changed and all your clothes are on the front lawn — on fire, *chances are you're having an argument.*

8. If your favorite bowling trophy lies decapitated, upside down in your fish tank, *chances are you're having an argument.*

9. If you were expecting a Valentine's Day card and instead receive a restraining order, *chances are you're having an argument.*

10.   If she accidentally drives over your new golf clubs — five times in a row, *chances are you're having an argument.*

11.   If she tells you, "Can you move a little to the left? Ah! Now you're in the range of my laser scope!", *chances are you're having an argument.*

12.   If she greets you at the door slinging nun-chucks, *chances are you're having an argument.*

13.   If he goes out for a pack of cigarettes in May and doesn't come back until July, and he doesn't even smoke, *chances are you're having an argument.*

HOW TO DRESS FOR AN ARGUMENT

Men and women don't realize just how important it is to dress for an argument. It is imperative that each person dress properly for the occasion.

Men

Men should dress in combat fatigues, though camouflage is tricky. If he is arguing in the living room, his fatigues should blend in with the carpet, sofa and drapes. Bandoleer rows of machine-gun bullets are a nice accessory, and should in no way be considered gaudy or gauche. The wearing of high, possibly hip-length boots are encouraged, since the B.S. will be plentiful and deep. Above all, he should be wearing a titanium cup impermeable to knives, bullets, and high heels.

Women

Women should dress comfortably with little regard for attire, since her twelve attack dogs will be doing most of the fighting. For the woman who is insistent on making a fashion statement, however, she may choose to be dressed in a bullet-proof jump

suit equipped with several pockets and back straps to carry mace, TNT, cross-bow, bungy cords, blow torch, and mascara (make sure there is always ample cleavage showing for distraction).

THE FIVE F'S IN AN ARGUMENT

There are five stances that individuals can take in an argument.

Fight   The most popular of the stances. This is when both parties "duke it out" using boxing gloves, verbal abuse, or the good china.

Flight   This is when, during the argument, one of you books a red-eye flight to Rio de Janeiro.

Fake   This is when one of you gets a "double" to take your place in the argument, while you search for someone that's easier to live with.

Fold   This is when the loser of the argument has to fold the laundry for a week.

Fuck It!   This is when one of you gets tired of these pointless battles and becomes gay.

CHAPTER 10

HOW TO LOSE POINTS
WITH THE OPPOSITE SEX

Since men and women haven't the slightest clue as to what each other wants, being successful at pleasing each other is totally out of the question. Therefore, the next best thing is to lose as few points as possible, unless you have declared war, in which case you want to lose as *many* points as possible *(see Chapter 12, How To Wage War)*.

WAYS MEN *THINK* THEY ARE SCORING POINTS WITH A WOMAN

Losing points should be a conscious, premeditated activity. Nevertheless, since most men are unconscious, they need to lose points inadvertently. Here are a few ways:

1. Buy her discounted clothes marked "irregular", pointing out that a third sleeve can come in handy if you lose one of the other two.

2. Since women enjoy an aesthetic, decorative atmosphere, arrange your empty beer cans in an eye-catching pyramid-like structure as a dining room table centerpiece.

3. Buy her chocolates the day *after* Valentine's Day. Explain you were able to buy twice as much because they were half the price.

4. When you take her to a restaurant that actually uses tablecloths, magnanimously tell her that even though she will be paying for her half, you will be leaving the tip.

5. On the other hand, when taking her to the Monster Truck Exhibition, always offer to pay. However, ask her to spring for the beer, which should generally run more than the tickets.

6. Show how much you appreciate her family by saying things like, "God, your sister is hot!"

7. Show her how hygienic you are; flush the toilet after you're done.

8. Be considerate. When you ask her to get you a beer, suggest she also get one for herself.

9. Don't criticize her for forgetting things at the supermarket. Help her with little notes such as, "Out of Doritos" or "Low on Budweiser".

10. On her birthday use deodorant.

11. Buy her sexy lingerie. Then wear it for her at the dinner table.

12. Send her a love poem, possibly one that starts with, "There was an Old Man from Nantucket..."

13. When watching TV together, reduce your channel surfing in half — from 40 channels in 10 seconds to 20 channels in 10 seconds.

14. When watching a romantic movie on TV together, hold in your gas until the commercial.

15. Spell "I love you" with your little shaving hairs in the bathroom sink.

16. Empathize with her pregnant condition by wearing a bowling ball in your pants.

17. When offering your words of wisdom, waive your consulting fee.

18. Wipe off your secretary's lipstick before entering the house.

19. Encourage her to talk as much as possible. Record her 4-day Nag-a-thon on video tape for a Guinness Book World Record.

20. When you get caught, explain that the woman you are having an affair with is only superior in breast size, not intelligence.

21. When she complains you are avoiding issues, tell her you'll talk about it later.

22. If she charges at you with a carving knife, be sensitive; ask if she's upset.

23. Likewise, when you are tossing steak knives into the dishwasher from across the room, let her know that you missed her.

24. If she's feeling vulnerable and depressed, cheer her up by wearing a "Big Bird" condom.

25. When you are trying to give her an orgasm, only glance at your watch *once*.

26. In the bathroom leave the seat down. Urinate in the shower.

WAYS WOMEN *THINK* THEY ARE SCORING POINTS WITH MEN

1. Since men love competition, tell him how many more orgasms your girlfriends are getting from their men.

2. Make a special dinner for him. Take a frozen entree out of the aluminum container and place it on a fancy floral paper plate.

3. When he asks you to sew the buttons on his shirts, offer, instead, to thread the needle.

4. Set aside a special room where he can smoke his pipes and cigars to his heart's content — the shed.

5. Show how agreeable you can be. Half the time *you* do what you want, and the other half have *him* do what you want.

6. Praise him at every opportunity. Marvel how something so small could feel so good.

7. Men love a good sense of humor. Giggle the first time you see his penis.

8. Never whine that the blindfold is too tight or that the ropes are cutting into your wrists.

9. Men love challenging assemblies, so buy your new two-bedroom country home as a knock-down do-it-yourself assembly kit. Make sure you throw away the directions.

10. Men love surprises, so don't tell him about your positive pregnancy test until your second trimester.

11. Don't tax a man's memory. Call him at work six or seven times a day to remind him what groceries to bring home.

12.   Be considerate. Avoid giving him oral sex while wearing braces.

13.   When he threatens to leave you for good, offer to help him pack.

14.   Tell him he can "have his way with you" — right after he paints your five-bedroom house.

15.   Even though you make him wait 50 dates before you sleep with him, "give him a little more" each time.

11

COMMUNICATING DIFFICULT FEELINGS
WITH THE HATE LETTER

When we are lovey-dovey, kissy-facey, touchy-feely, and koochy-kooey, it's hard to get down to the real **nitty-gritty.** It's hard to give your partner that smack in the face you know they deserve. But it's important to let them "have it" once in a while, even if it's just to wipe that silly smile off their face.

....

When we are lovey-dovey, kissy-facey, touchy-feely, and koochy-kooey, it's hard to get down to the real nitty-gritty.

....

Sometimes, however, communicating words of disgust and revulsion don't seem to get the attention they deserve. That's why it's important to put your thoughts in writing. This way your partner can read your vitriolic invective over and over again.

The best way to do this is with the Hate Letter.

THE HATE LETTER TECHNIQUE

By getting rid of our superficial emotions, eventually we get down to the core issues that are really pissing us off. There are several parts to this process.

Purging Superficial Emotions

1. Write down any positive feelings you may have about the other person. Then slap your palm to your forehead and say, "Yeah, right!"

2. Throw the paper away and write down what you really think of the asshole.

3. Write down how you think your partner will respond revengefully to your raging rant.

4. Tell your partner to have intercourse with him or herself — though not necessarily in those terms.

5. Share your Hate Letter with your lawyer.

6. Then write a Hate Letter to your lawyer.

STEP 1: WRITING THE HATE LETTER

1. Address the letter to your partner appropriately. Use "To Whom It May Concern". If you have been living together for some time, use "Dear Current Occupant".

2. Start writing your feelings of dislike and disappointment. Continue with your feelings of misery and unhappiness. Then write down your feelings of scorn and disgust. Follow up with feelings of hate and loathing. Proceed

with feelings of annihilation and decapitation. Progress to chop and puree. Include how you would like to put their face in a Cuisinart, their ears in a vice grip, and their ass in a wood chipper (Be hygienic. Sterilize all equipment to prevent an infection.).

3. Keep writing until feelings of hate run out. This may take a while — several months or years. Notice if the seasons have changed from when you first began the letter. See if the pages of the calendar flip by like in those old movies.

4. Sign the letter at the end. Make up a name and use it as an alias. Keep changing your alias every three months.

THE HATE LETTER FORMAT

Use the format below when thinking about what to say. Complete each sentence. Show all work on a separate piece of paper. Do not cheat by reading the divorce proceedings of the person living next to you.

To simplify writing your Hate Letters, you may wish to make copies of this page and use it as a guide for your own Hate Letters. Generally, the most releasing expressions are: "I am sad", "I am disillusioned", "I regret", and "I hate your fucking guts". It usually takes about twenty minutes to write a Hate Letter, but you'll find it becomes a lot faster the more Hate Letters you write.

A Hate Letter

Simply fill in the sample outline below in any way that is most damaging.

Dear: (choose one) putz, pinhead, dork dangler, fartface, fuckface, jerkoff, shitball, shithead, dipshit, shit-for-brains, moron, numbskull, nitwit, halfwit, dimwit, witless wonder, dingbat, bird brain, dumb cluck, nincompoop, schmuck, smartass, jackass, bigass, halfass, asshole, asswipe, cretin, twit, twerp, or smegma-sucking scumbag:

Date: (later than you think)_____

I am writing this letter to unleash my feelings of revulsion for you.

For Anger

- I don't like it...*when you're around.*

- I feel frustrated...*I can't make you disappear.*

- I am angry that...*I convinced myself I liked you.*

- I feel annoyed...*at every damn thing you do.*

- I want...*nothing to do with you.*

For Sadness

- I feel disappointed...*I dumped a dentist for you.*

- I am sad that...*I lost his number.*

- I feel hurt...*every time you used the handcuffs.*

- I wanted...*something way better than you.*

- I want...*you to get lost.*

For Fear

- I feel worried...*the next person I'm with will find out I dated you.*

- I am afraid...*you gave me an infection.*

- I feel scared...*that it hasn't gone away.*

- I need...*antibiotics.*

- I want...*a second opinion.*

For Regret

- I feel embarrassed...*you saw me naked.*

- I am sorry...*I ever met you.*

- I feel ashamed...*people saw us in public.*

- I didn't want...*our affair to get out.*

- I want... *to enter the witness protection program.*

For Hate

- I hate...*every molecule in your body.*

- I want...*to be hypnotized, to forget every sordid memory of you.*

- I understand...*my medication caused temporary insanity.*

- I forgive...*your mother for giving birth to you.*

- I appreciate...*your leaving for Zimbabwe.*

- I thank you for...*not having "spring-offs" with me,
     thereby propagating your line of genetic
     mutants and mental deficients.*

- I know...*better now.*

A Typical Hate Letter

Daphne phoned her husband, Cedric, at his office to tell him to bring home some important mail. Cedric was busy in the copy room at the time with his secretary and never heard the phone ring since something was covering his ears. When Cedric got home, without the mail of course, Daphne let him have it — up his rear end with a hot curling iron!

Instead of dumping his defensive feelings on her and ruining his evening, he decided to write Daphne a Hate Letter.

This is Cedric's Hate Letter:

Dear Daphne:

Anger: I am so angry I even came home.

Sadness: I could have stayed with my secretary for a few
               more hours.

Fear: I'm afraid you'll catch me sooner or later, I only
               wish I gave a shit.

Regret: Boy, I wish I were single again — babes, booze
               and the Bahamas! Now it's bitching, belly-aching,
               and bullshit.

Hate: How do I hate thee? Let me count the ways! I
               would hate having all my toenails ripped out and

then having hot lemon juice poured into the wounds, but compared to how much I hate being with you — the toenail thing would be a pleasure. You're worried about some stupid mail — probably your Neiman-Marcus catalog. Well, I got news for you. You're getting something in the mail real soon — a summons!

I Hate You,
Cedric

STEP 2: THE REVENGE LETTER

If your behated sends you a Hate Letter — strike back with a vengeance! The Revenge Letter is your retaliation to the Hate Letter.

A Typical Revenge Letter:

Daphne was not about to take Cedric's Hate Letter lying down. As a matter of fact, she had no intention of lying down for Cedric ever again! Here is Daphne's Revenge Letter:

Dear Cedric:

Insight: You two-timing worm. I know you're having an affair with that twenty-year-old twit you call a secretary because I've been having you tailed, you idiot!

Information: I've got more dirt on you than a Hoover Vacuum.

Action: While you were at work today — banging the bimbo — I cleaned out all our bank accounts, mutual funds, and IRA's. And all your clothes.

Advice: If I were you, I'd leave the country. You are screwed, blued, and tattooed.

Revenge: Watch for me on *Oprah* tomorrow. The topic? "Men Who Cheat On Their Wives, Lie On Their Income Tax Returns, Keep False Books, And The Women Who Hate Them". Oh yeah, then I'll be on *Sally*, *Geraldo*, *Hard Copy*, *Soft Copy* and *Xerox Copy*. And then....I'M CALLING YOUR MOTHER! Well, I have to go now and order that $3,000 vibrating lounge chair from Sharper Image — on your credit card. Ta, ta, pencil dick.

Gleefully,
Daphne

MINI HATE LETTERS

If you are upset and don't have twenty minutes or more to write a Hate Letter, you can try writing a mini Hate Letter. Here are some examples:

Example 1

Dear Henry:

I am angry that you think my nipples are dials on a short-wave radio. Every time you touch me I feel like a human Etch-A-Sketch. Caress my nipples nicely, or I'm going to cut off your fingers and arc-weld your ass shut!

Pissed off,
Petunia

Example 2

Dear Rosemary:

I hate having to look at your pathetic excuses for cooking. It's not that I mind eating Spam kabobs smothered in Velveeta on a bed of Beefaroni — but just once I'd like food that doesn't have enough nitrates to kill off an entire colony of laboratory rats!

Nauseously,
Norman

Example 3

Dear Billy Bob:

You may think I enjoy sitting here in the living room holding an umbrella over my head, but I really think you should fix the trailer roof. Not tomorrow after the tractor pulls, or Tuesday after the fussball tournament, or Wednesday after your lodge meeting. NOW! You shiftless, beer-guzzling, chili-eating, chili-farting, monster-truck-watching, pants-below-the-ass-crack-wearing, redneck sumabitch!

> *I ain't shittin',*
> *Sue-Ellen*

We hope you will use this Hate Letter technique. The Hate Letter has transformed the lives of mildly unhappy, somewhat discontented individuals into actively miserable, decidedly suicidal degenerates.

....

The Hate Letter has transformed the lives of mildly unhappy, somewhat discontented individuals into actively miserable, decidedly suicidal degenerates.

....

WHAT TO DO IF YOUR PARTNER CAN'T READ

It is difficult to send a Hate Letter to your partner if he or she can't read. If they can't read "run Spot, run", how are they going to understand "die Shithead, die!". It is not unusual to find that the only letter of the alphabet your partner can read is the letter "X" where they had to sign as an illegal alien.

Nevertheless, there are many schools that teach "hate mime", where you can learn to communicate your hate nonverbally. You can also hone your skills through "hate charades", where your partner can piece together your threats one word at a time.

Hand gestures are also effective. Most of these are quite recognizable. If, however, they still don't understand the upward extension of the middle finger, tell them to just go #$%@¢& themselves!

WAYS WE COVER UP OUR FEELINGS

For Men

Men often hide their feelings by feeling other feelings. For instance, men may use *anger* as a way of avoiding feelings of *loathsome disgust*. Then they will *regret* that they got *angry* which will make them feel *irritated* and *guilty*. Once they realize they are feeling *guilty*, they will feel *shame* and *embarrassment* that they felt *guilty*. Realizing they are feeling *embarrassed* they will feel *pissed off* at their partners which will make them *feel like leaving* the relationship for good. Wanting to leave the relationship will make them *feel like a low-life coward* and they will want their blankie and warm milk. Realizing that their manliness has been reduced to the whimpering cries of a slobbering nebbish, they will *feel like a jerk*, which will then make them feel — *angry!* Realizing he is about to start this whole damn feeling process all over again, a man will *really feel like* polishing off a fifth of Jack Daniels!

For Women

Women deny their feelings by using the ever-popular one-word answer, "nothing".

For example, a man may see a woman curled up in the fetal position, wearing old sweat pants, stabbing the floor with a steak knife, muttering over and over to herself, "Why was I born? Why was I born? Why was I born?"

He will ask her, "Honey what's wrong?" She will roll her bloodshot eyes back into her head, bare her fangs, and reply, "nothing". Basically, when a woman says nothing she means *something*. Or she could mean *everything*. Then she will feel *confusion*. Is it *something* or is it *everything*? Then she will feel *eight years old* because she can't remember the answer. She will then look at herself, lying on the floor in old sweat pants holding a steak knife, and figure she will probably lean more towards the *everything* side. She will then feel *triumph* now that she's discovered her life is a *total mess*. This knowledge will make her feel *hungry*, prompting her to open up a can of barbecue Pringle's which she will eat in one sitting. Afterwards, she will feel *guilt* and *shame* and will stare, *weeping* at her thighs for 20 minutes, expecting them to immediately expand. When the man, upon seeing her in this pathetic state, asks her what's wrong, she will reply, "nothing".

What can a man do about this?

Nothing.

12

KEEPING THE WAR RAGING, NOW AND FOREVER

Sometimes love and hate will alternate
You're feeling good, then not so great
Should you go make love or go make hate?
Neither! Just stay home and masturbate!

This famous poem, written by an anonymous sperm donor, typifies the dilemma we face every day in our romantic lives — the back and forth's, the to's and fro's, the yin's and yang's, the Lucy's and Ricky's of our emotional existence. When we're in love, our moods can change faster than the time slots opposite Seinfeld.

THE EMOTIONAL ROLLER COASTER

Relationships change constantly. They are a cross between a roller-coaster, a merry-go-round, and a Roto-Rooter suck-vac. Somehow, some way, there's always some shit hitting the fan.

One minute he's up — the next minute he's down. Twenty minutes later he's up, the next minute he's down. One minute she's sullen and depressed, the next minute she's sullen and depressed. Three weeks later she's still sullen and depressed — though this time with a different man. So we can see just how volatile these mood swings can be.

....

Relationships change constantly. They are a cross between a roller-coaster, a merry-go-round, and a Roto-Rooter suck-vac.

....

RELATIONSHIPS CHANGE MINUTE BY MINUTE

Nothing stays the same in relationships — other than perpetual discontent. That always remains constant. For example:

One minute you can't imagine not loving your partner.
The next minute you can't imagine not loving your secretary or personal trainer.

....

Nothing stays the same in relationships — other than perpetual discontent. That always remains constant.

....

One minute you are attracted to your partner.
The next minute they make a commitment and you book the red-eye to Costa del Sol.

One minute he's passionate and aroused.
The next minute he's snoring.

One minute in the middle of the night you have the affair of a lifetime.
The next minute you're wondering how to get the asshole out of your bed.

One minute you are overflowing with generosity.
The next minute they eat one of your Reese's Peanut Butter Cups and you call the cops to press charges.

....

No matter what you do about it, unresolved issues come up like onion breath after a bad chili dog.

....

One minute you want to spend the rest of your life with your partner.
The next minute you think, "If I spend two more minutes with this putz, I'll need a Lithium-Xanax-Prozac cocktail."

No matter what you do about it, unresolved issues come up like onion breath after a bad chili dog. It all comes up — all the shit you whine about in therapy and out of therapy. But the secret to dealing with it is learning the fine art of blame.

HOW TO BLAME YOUR PARTNER FOR JUST ABOUT EVERYTHING

The 99/1 Principle

In relationships, like politics, you always need a scapegoat; and who better than your partner? That's right, if it weren't for them you wouldn't be in the predicament you're in now. Let's face it, if you were by yourself all the time, the worst that would happen would be you developed a mild rash from touching yourself with dirty hands. Big deal.

We call this the 99/1 Principle because when things go wrong, your partner should bear 99% of the blame. When things go right, you should claim 99% of the credit. You could actually claim 100% of the credit, but giving 1% away makes you appear humble. If you are single and don't have a partner, *always blame your parents.*

For some blaming is easy. Some people are born blamers because they blame so naturally and effortlessly. And when you think about it — who can blame them?

For others blaming is hard work and requires practice and exercise as well as creative thinking.

Fill in The Blanks

To help you get started, to help you recall all the bad, disgusting, insensitive things that *you* did which you want to blame on your partner, fill in the blanks.

If it weren't for my partner

_____.

If it weren't for my partner

_____.

If it weren't for my partner

_____.

If it weren't for my partner

_____.

If it weren't for my partner

_____.

If you are having trouble with this exercise, you are not stretching the truth far enough.

For example, let's take the statement, "If it weren't for my partner, I wouldn't be on death row pleading for a pardon from the Governor." Think about it.

The reason you are on death row is because you tortured and murdered your third-grade teacher, Sister Mary "knuckleslammer" O'Leary. At gun point you made her write down, "I must not talk during study hall" 3 million times, forced her to chew gum, and tell the same knock-knock joke 8 million times. Since she was diabetic and the gum was not sugarless, she died of a stroke, and the police caught you shredding the 3 million lines because a neighbor complained of hearing the same knock-knock joke 8 million times.

But why did you go to murder your third-grade teacher? Well, you were in a movie theater with some of your friends, and you asked one of them to pass the popcorn. The usher heard you and said, "You must not talk." This reminded you of your third-grade teacher, Sister Mary "knuckleslammer" O'Leary. You then became insanely enraged and had to murder her.

But why did you go to the movie theater with your friends? Well, you were supposed to be in Chicago for a business convention, but you missed the plane. So you canceled the trip and went to the movies with your friends.

But why did you miss the plane? Well, you were driving to the airport and you didn't get more than three blocks away before your car overheated, causing you to miss the plane.

But why did your car overheat? Well, you forgot to put oil in the engine, which caused the car to overheat.

But why did you forget to put oil in the engine? Simple, because when you were driving, you were thinking about the character, "Chewbacca", from *Star Wars*, instead of paying attention to the red warning light on your dash board. This caused you to forget about the oil.

But why were you thinking about Chewbacca from Star Wars? Simple, because you were watching a television show with your partner one night, and you changed the channel to catch the score of the Lakers game. When you switched channels, your partner moaned loudly which reminded you of Chewbacca from *Star Wars* which made you forget the oil, which caused your car to overheat, which caused you to miss your trip to Chicago, which caused you to go to the movies with your friends, which caused you to be "shushed" by the usher, which caused you to murder your third-grade teacher, Sister Mary "knuckleslammer" O'Leary.

So it's pretty clear that,

If it weren't for my partner, I wouldn't be on death row.

See, it's easy.

The next step after blaming your partner is to wage war against them. This can also follow a fight-to-the-death argument (see Chapter 9).

HOW TO WAGE WAR

Waging war is the most important part of getting even in your relationships. People naively think that relationships are about compatibility, until they soon find out they are really about *combatibility.*

....

People naively think that relationships are about compatibility, until they soon find out they are really about *combatibility.*

....

Even so, many people believe they are skilled war mongers when, in fact, they are amateur cry babies. Waging war requires professional know-how, not amateur whining and finger pointing.

HOW AMATEURS WAGE WAR

You can always tell amateur war waging by its most striking characteristic — *it's been done!* For decades and decades fighting couples use the same hackneyed techniques serving only to prolong their sickening stalemate, rather than to nail a decisive victory. Typical ways amateurs wage war are:

- Write a tell-all biography about your partner. Tell all lies!

- Promote the book on every tacky talk show and TV tabloid.

- Expose your partner's fetish for hot-pink latex bonnets with chin straps.

- File paternity suits, custody suits, slander suits, 3-piece suits.

- Sue for alimony, palimony, and matrimony, even if you've only had one date.

- Accuse your partner of every type of abuse, especially "self-abuse".

- Accuse your partner of impotence.

- Then accuse your partner of nymphomania.

- Just accuse your partner of everything.

These techniques have proven themselves to be sophomoric. Worse than that, they're *freshmanic!*

HOW PROFESSIONALS WAGE WAR

Professionals know that men and women require different strategies and tactics for doing battle.

Declaring War On A Man

A woman must realize that men are creatures of habit. They eat, propagate, and watch television. To properly declare war you must sabotage his basic needs through the strategic use of *womaneuvers*. To do this you must:

- Withhold food

- Withhold sex

- Hide the remote

Let's examine the above. By **withholding food** we mean just don't cook! Most guys can't even make a salad without causing something to burn. Unless you cook, he will be forced to eat potato chips, Doritos, beer nuts, and month-old Chinese food. After this gourmet buffet runs out, he will become helpless and weak. He'll be as spineless as spaghetti. You will be able to take his check book right out of his pants without any struggle.

Withholding sex, when coupled with withholding food, will make him the man voted most likely to concede. You'll call him "caterpillar" because every time he comes over to you he'll be crawling.

Finally, bring out the heavy artillery. **Hide the remote** and watch your man quickly go berserk. What will he do without WWF? Hockey? Soccer? Football? Baseball? Those 900 numbers? Without television a man will be forced to read, think, or, God forbid, *talk!* It will be the end of his life as he knows it. He would even commit suicide, if he wasn't so scared-to-death of killing himself! Soon he will be holding up the white flag and you will be holding up a new dress.

Declaring War on a Woman

Women are vain and vulnerable creatures. To properly declare war on a woman you must:

- Hide her charge cards

- Hide her makeup

- Rig the bathroom scale

When you **hide her charge cards**, a woman will be forced to find other leisure activities besides shopping to fill her time. She will wander aimlessly for several days, or stare drooling at the Home Shopping Network since *she has no other leisure activities besides shopping!*

When you **hide her makeup** you freeze her in her tracks. She can't go out of the house without "putting on her face". You can leave your outboard motor running on the living room rug and hang your jockstrap from the chandelier in the dining room. But when she irately asks you to remove them say, "Do it yourself, your Royal Bitchness." She'll chase you with a butcher knife, but when you run out the door, she won't be able to follow. To a woman, facing the public without makeup is like sunbathing to a vampire — it's the kiss of death.

Then, the coup d'état. **Rig the bathroom scale** to always read five pounds over. This is the most diabolical form of warfare. Mustard gas and nerve gas pale in comparison. The woman will be so depressed, when she gets on the scale, she will cry for a week asking everybody in sight if she looks fat. This is the optimum time to take advantage of her weakness and make her sign a surrender agreement with clauses for all-night card games, week-long fishing trips, and oral sex on demand.

THE SEASONS OF HATE

Relationships are like compost. They take a lot of time to break down and decay before they finally rot and putrefy. To keep the war raging forever, we need to be able to understand the many facets of hate and the many seasons it goes through in order to not only survive, but to get even and wreak revenge.

The Springtime of Discontent

People think that winter is the time of our discontent. It would be nice if it took that long. But our discontent begins as soon as we see the loser that our best friend fixed us up with on a blind date. Springtime is a time of innocence, at least until proven guilty by a court of law.

....

Springtime is a time of innocence, at least until proven guilty by a court of law.

....

The Summer is When Things Really Start Heating Up

You're hot to trot. Your partner makes you sizzle. Just the sight of them makes your whole body heat up in a frenzy. Then you realize … you forgot to turn on the air conditioner. Let's face it. The hot, sweaty summer is not the season for body heat, it's the season for *body odor!*

The Fall Is When Your Relationship Falls Apart Completely

The trees start to lose their leaves and you start to lose your patience. Then your partner loses the tan that made them look ten pounds thinner. All those little things you found so endearing during the heat waves of summer, now annoy the living shit out of you. You find yourself saying things like, "Hey! Do you have to breathe all the time? That in and out sound — it's so repetitious!" Then there's waking up next to your partner every morning thinking, "Dammit — you're still here!"

You find yourself saying things like, "Hey! Do you have to breathe all the time? That in and out sound — it's so repetitious!"

The Winter Begins a Cold War That Lasts Forever

Women sink into the pits and men go to the couch and everything turns to shit. Everyone feels gross and fat because it's winter. And what's the point — why dress up? It's 20 below outside. Everybody's bored and cold. There's lots of fights because neither partner wants to be the one to go out and get more ho-ho's, yoo-hoos, ding-dongs or vodka. So everyone broods in their corner and no one gets laid. It's too exhausting, what with taking off all those layers of clothes.

WAGING THE WAR FOREVER

Sustaining this kind of battle takes a special kind of hero — one that is strong, courageous, yet still missing a few oars in the water. It takes perseverance, it takes fortitude, and it takes a great deal of money for legal expenses. But in the end it's worth it. They've gotten their just desserts — and after all those desserts, their ends are starting to show it!

Yes, you have gotten your revenge and you may now declare victory and move on! Nothing can stop you now — nothing except a depressing call from your mother telling you, "You're not getting any younger or cuter, you know, and maybe you should just stop being so picky and settle down." So don't answer the phone! Keep marching through the seasons towards that rich reward that is yours — FREEDOM! FREEDOM! Freedom from nagging. Freedom from whining. Freedom from divorce proceedings, custody battles, and paternity suits.

May you find that one place that is truly the source of relationship freedom — solitary confinement in a maximum-security prison!

Live long and prosper.

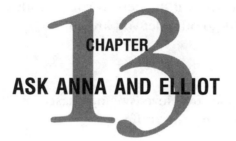

CHAPTER 13

ASK ANNA AND ELLIOT

Dear Anna and Elliot:

I get many different opinions about when it is proper to have sex in the dating process. Could you help me?

Dick

Dear Dick:

Always have sex *before* the first date. This way you don't spend a lot of time and money on someone who doesn't put out or who is bad in bed.

A & E

❋ ❋ ❋ ❋ ❋ ❋

Dear Anna & Elliot:

I want to ask my girlfriend to marry me. Would she be touched if I got down on one knee while proposing?

Jake

Dear Jake:

Yes. However, if your girlfriend got down on all fours, she could be touched even more.

A & E

✳ ✳ ✳ ✳ ✳ ✳

Dear Anna and Elliot:

How do you know if the person you're with is "the one"? Do alarms or sirens go off to let you know?

Gerard

Dear Gerard:

Not unless your true love is being chased by the police. You'll only know who "the one" is if :

1. You can go four straight hours without speed-slapping them and

2. Your mother *disapproves* of them.

Then you can be sure they're the one for you!

A & E

✳ ✳ ✳ ✳ ✳ ✳

Dear Anna & Elliot:

What do guys really want? I mean *really* want? I am so tired of trying to figure this out, my head hurts.

Penny

Dear Penny:

Guys want — what they can't have.

A & E

✳ ✳ ✳ ✳ ✳ ✳

Dear Anna and Elliot:

I drive a GEO. Will I ever get laid?

Sammy

Dear Sammy:
    Not a chance.

A & E

* * * * * *

Dear Anna & Elliot:
    How long is oral sex supposed to last before you feel like you're going to snap? The other night I was giving my boyfriend oral sex, and it seemed like it was taking forever. But when I peeked at the clock — only five minutes had passed! Do other women feel this way?

Vicki

Dear Vicki:
    That's why it's called a blow *job* instead of a blow *fun* or a blow *joy*. There will always be that work ethic involved. Get used to it.

A & E

* * * * * *

Anna Collins

Anna Collins is a stand-up comedienne, free-lance writer, and award-winning photographer. She has been seen on

VH-1's *Standup Spotlight*, *A&E's Girls' Night Out*, the *Rolonda Show*, and at major comedy clubs throughout the country. She currently lives in New York City. When she isn't writing or performing, she's hard at work keeping the cellulite off her thighs.

Elliot Sullivan

Elliot Sullivan is a stand-up comic, writer, therapist, and publisher. He has appeared on *Showtime's Comedy Club Network* and *The Everyday Show With Joan Lunden*. He holds

two degrees from Cornell University and he is a licensed trainer and co-developer of NLP. He currently resides in New York City. Never married, he is proof that these survival strategies can be applied successfully. Nevertheless, he keeps his weight down just in case he's been wrong all this time.